Alms for the Poor

Alms for the Poor

Copyright © Nathaniel Schellhase Hvizdos
Product of the United States of America
First Printing 2019, All Rights Reserved
Greenback Books (ain't no thing)
natetwostars@gmail.com
Instagram: @natetwostars

All Rights Reserved. No part of this book can be reproduced or transmitted in any form or by any means, graphic, electronic, or mechanical, including photocopying, recording, taping, or by any informational storage or retrieval system without written permission from the author.

©2019 Nathaniel Schellhase Hvizdos

ISBN - 9781704841892

**Dedicated
To
Dr. Frank Jenkins**

Alms for the Poor

PREFACE

**You sick of it all
Say you are hardcore
Listen to the knock
It's GOD at your door**

Alms for the Poor

Nathaniel Schellhase Hvizdos

INTRODUCTION
A True Short Story about a Child in an Adult Prison

James Montgomery Manuel
John 3:16
"For GOD so loved the world, that he gave his only begotten Son, that whosoever believeth in him should not perish, but have everlasting life."

Nathaniel Schellhase Hvizdos

Chapter One
Tears in my eyes

Richmond, Virginia ... Circa 1983;

I remember it was so hot that nobody in our crew had shirts on, a group of 17 youngsters, ranging in age between 14 and 16. We joked and laughed so hard with and at each other, I remember having tears in my eyes ... July was on fire but the fun we were having seemed to make the day cooler. We were all hanging out on "The Bench" at "The Rec" ... "The Bench" was a very long picnic bench which could seat at least 25 to 30 people and "The Rec" was short for Recreational Center; Every housing project in the city of Richmond had a "Rec" ... this one was located in the Creighton Court housing projects.

One of our crew members, "Fat Kevin" had a large radio/ cassette player which we called a "Beat Box" and he was blasting "Sucker MC's", by Run-D.M.C. ... when the song first came on, everyone, on one accord started repeating the words at the top of our lungs ...

"Two years ago, a friend of mine
Asked me to say some MC rhymes
So I said this rhyme I'm about to say
The rhyme was Def a-then it went this way
Took a test to become an MC
And Orange Krush became amazed at me
So Larry put me inside his Cad-illac
The chauffeur drove off and we never came back ..."

Almost as if on cue, someone pulled some flattened cardboard boxes from underneath "The Bench" and we all took turns "Break Dancing" and "Pop Locking". Then it seemed again, as if on cue, a crew of girls started showing up to watch. I remember how I felt when they arrived. I had a feeling of being on stage and performing just for one of the girls in particular.

Her name was Vonda and at 17 years old, she was so pretty, I declare, back then I thought she was some type of angel. Her skin looked like GOD mixed some honey, brown sugar and caramel in a giant bowl and dipped her in it; her smile was so perfect that when she laughed, I could've swore she had a set of sugar coated pearls for teeth. Her hair was long and looked so soft like beautiful black cotton.

But, the most amazing things about Vonda was how smart and confident she was. She was the leader of her crew and she was tougher than nails! Every time, without fail, when the dancing was over, she would come up to me and start talking to me. I recalled that I never knew just what to say. I was absolutely at a loss for words around her, but she never let that prevent her from kicking it with me.

While we exchanged a few laughs and a little ghetto gossip, Vonda asked me, right out of the blue, "You know you belong to me, right?" I was so shocked, I looked around to see who she was talking to ... then she asked me again. I knew she couldn't have been talking to me because I was, in my mind, completely out of her league ... In my crew, I was certainly not the toughest, I was not the smartest by far and on top of all that, at 14 years old, I was still, solidly a virgin. I responded saying something stupid like, "I don't know" ... I'll never forget the way she took my hand and gently began to walk with me away from the crowd.

Vonda looked at me while we strolled and said, "You're my man so you gotta start acting like it."

I recall saying to myself, "What the hell am I gonna do now? ... I don't know how to do that or be that!" So, I just replied "Okay" ... Right at that moment, we heard a scream coming from near the entrance of The Rec ... someone in our crew. It was Red Kenny's 12 year-old sister was being physically assaulted by a really big older guy from another housing project.

He was cowardly retaliating against her because her oldest brother had recently testified against the assailant's father in a huge drug trial. My entire crew rushed over to stop him and during our intercession, the guy was knocked completely unconscious. After we realized he was out cold, we all scattered. The next day in school 17 people from my crew were rounded up by detectives from the Richmond Police Department's robbery division. Apparently, the guy who we knocked out, reported to the authorities that someone had gone into his pocket while he was incapacitated and stole

his money.
	Nobody would confess to the crime so my whole crew was charged with robbery by mob. We were all tried as adults and each of us were sentenced to serve 8 years in The Virginia Department of Corrections (ADULT DIVISION).

Chapter Two
Seventeen Children

	We all remained in the local jail for 3 months after our sentencing. We were each given a cell and were separated from the local jail's general population.
	When the three months were up, one morning around 4:30 am, we were all put in handcuffs and our ankles were cuffed and chained. We were placed on a large armored bus and taken to Southampton Correctional Center in Capron, Virginia, roughly about 70 miles away from the city of Richmond.
	Capron, Virginia is the exact same place where Nathaniel Turner was hanged, beheaded and his head was impaled on a stake in front of the county's courthouse. All the children were told this by the prison's Captain, while we were in intake, being issued our prison clothes, bedding and prison numbers.
	The captain told us that number was our new name and that we must remember it at all times. I became known as prisoner number "143709". We were then escorted by three guards to the "chow hall", we were ordered to sit on some benches about fifteen feet in front of the building. The guards left us alone on the benches and we could hear the voices of men in the building who were looking at us through doors and windows with bars on them. They were absolutely frantic. They were saying things to us as if they were talking to females. I remember, literally pinching my arm, expecting to be awakened from my nightmare.
	The guards returned, one of them unlocked the doors to the building and ordered us to go inside, as we started walking single file into the building, I was third in the line, when I crossed the door seal I saw a sea of men who were in two distinct categories, "GORILLA" and "BEAR". The men were still saying vulgar and perverse things to us. We knew that the guards could hear what the men were saying to us but the guards didn't protest one bit,

in fact they were completely silent. It appeared that the biggest prisoners were the most vicious in their speech.

We went through a line to get our food and then sat down to eat. I recall that none of the children could eat one bite of food, not even the toughest kids in our group could eat. We were beyond terrified. When "chow" was ended the guards escorted all of the kids to general population and assigned each child a single cell.

The guards locked us in and walked away. I couldn't sleep because I knew it was just a matter of time before the men would run into the cell and attack me ... It never happened and I fell asleep.

Chapter Three
The Prison Yard

While he was slamming his keys against the cell door he said, "Get your little ass up, it's time for breakfast."

Now this group of guards seemed meaner than the guards from the day before. These guards were different in every way. They weren't silent like the other guards. They were saying vulgar things to us like the prisoners were.

We walked into the "chow hall" building the same way as the first time but the men were now getting in our space. They wouldn't touch us, but they were getting up in our faces and the guards were smiling.

We were served our food and some of the kids managed to eat a little, I managed to take a few bites of eggs. After breakfast was over, we were taken to the prison yard ... it was a vast, huge and sprawling complex of sports facilities. State of the art in every sense of the word "STATE".

Unbeknownst to us at the time, the Virginia Department of Corrections had the most prolific and professional athletic leagues, comparably to other state and federal prisons all over the USA. Since the inception of state and federal prison sports leagues in the early 1920s.

Moreover, and specifically, Virginia's prisoners dominated and outperformed all other state and federal prison teams consecutively each year in Football, Baseball, Basketball and Boxing. The prisoners all gathered in the center of the prison yard, which was surrounded by a football field, a baseball diamond, a large building which housed a basketball court and next to that building was an outdoor boxing ring.

The children were escorted by the guards to an area directly in front of the boxing ring, there were men everywhere ... all of the bleachers (football, baseball and boxing) were so filled, they looked like they would collapse, even the fields were covered with prisoners. There was a group of thirteen prisoners who stood out in the crowd.

We soon discovered that these were the "shot callers" i.e. although they were convicts themselves, they governed the rest of the prisoners. I recalled noticing earlier that these men were the most-vilest, perverse and insulting in their speech towards the children when we were in the "Chow Hall."

I'll never forget how quiet it became. It was freezing cold and all one could see was the vapor of frost coming from all the men. The thirteen "Shot Callers" spoke to the crowd with one voice, they all spoke the same words in unison ... Their words will remain seared in my mind as long as I live, breathe and have my being on earth. This is what they said, "GOD sent us these children! to help them! Guide them! honor them! protect them! and teach them!"

When they were done speaking the crowd of men, guards and prisoners alike shouted in response like they had just seen a home run, or a touchdown, or a dunk or a knockout. The Shot Callers turned out to be the complete opposite of the vulgar, insulting and perverted monsters which they feigned to be initially. The guards also were really not who they appeared to be. Turned out that the Shot Callers were all Christians except one who was a Muslim ... they were all devout men of deep faith, impeccable integrity, iron discipline and amazingly powerful character.

They all spoke several languages. They each had committed the entire Bible and Quran to memory. These men were so eloquent that their mastery of the English language was nothing less than commending. "Able" Jackson was the top Shot Caller and he then asked the children did we want to get saved and hand our lives over to JESUS?

Each of us said yes and they commenced to praying the "Prayer of Salvation" with us. It was at that time that I instinctively knew that JESUS was real and that HE truly loved me. I can honestly say, I got saved for real that cold December morning in 1984. They didn't teach any of the children the fundamentals of football, basketball or baseball ... they taught all of the kids how to fight.

Chapter Four
No Rest For The Weary

After lunch, the children were escorted to the administrative building and given our work assignments. Some of us were placed on kitchen detail, some on housing unit cleaning detail and then others (myself included) were placed on "road gangs." I worked on Gang Eleven which conducted all of the grueling work of managing the acres and acres of farmland that the prison had its functioning on for over 100 years.

Each morning at exactly 4:00 am a horn would blast and the cell doors would be opened and all the prisoners would start going to breakfast one building at a time, when the meal was over we all reported to work.

My first day on Gang Eleven unfolded in this order. Twenty-five men and one boy were all placed in ankle cuffs which were connected by long chains, marshaled onto an armored bus and taken to a very wide field of large tree stumps. There were two guards armed with shot guns and a third guard armed with a pistol. The guard with the pistol handed us our work tools, an axe, shovel and a pick-axe. I was shown what to do in our task of "pulling up stumps" and then the back-breaking work began.

We worked until 12:30 and I declare, I never knew pain like that before or after. I felt like someone had beaten my entire body with a baseball bat. Absolutely demanding is an understatement as it related to my daily routine. Up at 4:00 am in the field at sun-up until 12:30.

After lunch, I went to school until 3:00. From school, we went to the yard for boxing training and then to dinner at 5:00. After dinner, we trained some more until lock down at 8:30. I recall collapsing in intense exhaustion every night when the cell doors were locked. Each morning, when we reached the field, our gang's inmate leader, "Rosco" ... an "old head," called such because of the twenty-nine years he had served on a life sentence ... would say to us, "There ain't no rest for the weary". On Saturdays, we trained all day and on Sundays, we went to Church.

The weekends also were the visiting days. I think back and recollect how comforted my mother was when I explained to her what my daily and weekly schedule was like in prison. But she always seemed to cry when it was time to go. My dad and my sisters were just as comforted as my mother was when I, essentially, let them know that I was doing alright inside.

Chapter Five
Hits Like a Mule Kicks

My first fight took place on the third day of June 1986 as a 142 lbs., lightweight novice during regional competition; men from every super maximum and maximum-security prison all over the state of Virginia came to Southampton Correctional Center to determine who would fight in the upcoming statewide competition. In every weight category, all of the champions were from Southampton C.C.. So, I had a tremendous amount of expectation on me from, not only my coaches but also from all of the men at the institution whom I represented ... as a matter of fact, history was being made because of our ages which was unprecedented as it related to our team membership and participation in the tournament.

The man whom I was scheduled to go three, two-minute rounds with was from the Virginia State Penitentiary, known as "The Wall" and located in Richmond, Virginia. It was one of the oldest prisons in America, having been established in 1800, and had housed the electric chair beginning in 1908; "The Wall" was considered to be one of the most dangerous and deadliest prisons in America.

I didn't know at the time, but my opponent was not an amateur at all, he had 37 wins 35 by way of knock-out 4 losses and 2 draws as a professional, but because there was nobody from Southampton C.C. in our weight class left to fight him except me. In addition to that, none of the other five lightweights from other institutions want- ed to fight him, because they were all undefeated and al- ready locked in to proceed to the impending state finals, they were unwilling to risk losing to him.

My coaches made an agreement with the judges for

me to fight him and from what I was told afterwards, one of my coaches assured the judges that I was able and said, "The boy hits like a mule kicks!" I was so nervous and scared that I thought for sure that my knees were going to start knocking together. Each time that I looked across the ring at my opponent, he looked completely re- laxed and totally at ease.

Coach Jack "The Hammer" Williams, must have told me a million times, "Son, keep your jab in his face and work your way inside and beat his body."

I nodded my head yes and went to the center of the ring to get instructions from the referee, after that we returned to our respective corners. Coach reminded meagain to keep my jab on him and work his body hard. The bell rang and we ran towards one another.

I got my jab off first and ducked a counter right hand from him and I managed to get off a really nice left hook to his body and doubled up with a perfect left hook to his chin. Then it seemed like everything was in slow motion as I watched the guy falling to the canvas. The referee ordered me to a neutral corner and my competitor got up to a standing eight count.

The ref asked him if he wanted to continue and he started shaking his head no, while blood poured out of his mouth. His corner men came out with the doctor to tend to him, but I wasn't moved by that as much as I was moved by the thunderous applause and shouts of celebration made by the hundreds of men in the bleachers.

Chapter Six
The Machine

Matthew, "Merciless" Johnson was the reigning and undisputed lightweight champion of professional prison boxing for eight long years. At 39 years old, 6'2 and 143 lbs., he was legendary for one thing, and one thing only, his perfect and impeccable record of 55 wins by way of knockout, 0 losses, 0 draws.

Matthew was in prison, serving life, for killing a man, with his bare hands, who raped his sister, he was rumored to have said on occasion, concerning the murder, "I got to that piece of shit before the police did." Merciless was one of the funniest men on earth, he was so funny, I believed that he could make a dog laugh. He worked closely with our coaching staff and was responsible for establishing the tradition, which dictated that all the light-weight fighters would only spar with heavyweight fighters.

    One day, Merciless was studying my sparing regimen with a 250 lbs. heavyweight teammate of ours when he yelled out, "That kid ain't human! He's a machine!"

    So, from that day foreword, they started calling me, James "The Machine" Manuel. Every month, twice a month, our team had bouts with other prisons throughout the state. I was, it seemed, in a perpetual state of excitement, amazement and sheer astonishment, because I kept winning - all by knockout in the first round.

    Merciless was at work in the kitchen one morning, slipped, fell and severely injured his back. He was scheduled to defend his title in two months and this unfortunate set of circumstances was tremendously troubling to our institution's superlative record. Coach, conferred with Merciless and both agreed that I would fight for the vacated lightweight title against another undefeated fighter from Powhatan Correctional Center, also known as the "State Farm" and more infamously known as the "Slaughter House", suitably named because of the high rates and instances of inmate stabbings.

    My team of twenty fighters arrived at the Slaughter House early in the morning on Saturday, May 9th 1987. I wasn't scared, frightened nor uneasy. I was totally horrified! I had heard so many gruesome accounts of men being stabbed to death at Powhatan Correctional Center.

    Coach Jack "The Hammer" Williams, who was serving a 250 year sentence for carrying out one of the longest running bank robbery sprees in America; he had completed doing 20 years in Federal penitentiary in 1979 and now was serving his state time; Coach had served a few years of his state sentence at Slaughter House before eventually being transferred to Southampton C.C. and when we arrived it seemed like he was having a family reunion with many of the convicts. They were overjoyed to see him.

    Coach just kept on bragging about me and in his words, "Baby boy is gonna keep the title where it's supposed to be."

I was in true bewilderment, for two reasons: one because coach was so friendly with these men who had gained infamy via violent and butchering killings, the second reason being the incredible confidence he had in my abilities. The weigh-in was in a huge gym and it was so many men there that it was literally, standing room only. Anthony "The Executioner", my opponent was the blackest person, I had ever seen. He was so black that he really looked blue. He weighed in at 142lbs but he was so muscular that he looked much heavier, he had extremely long arms and he towered over my 6'0 frame by 5 inches . What was so troubling about my competition is the fact that he didn't earn his ring name for what he had accomplished in the sport of boxing. I was heading into hand to hand com- bat with a professional killer. Coach must have sensed my fear because he began to tell me things like, "Son, this is going to be the easiest fight yet." ... "Son, this guy has never been tested by a hard-hitting fighter like you." and "You're one fight away from being the youngest lightweight champion in the his- tory of prison boxing". Honestly, none of what he said could alleviate my terror. The last fight that took place before the main event came and went so fast my head started spinning.

Then came the moment of truth. The loud speaker started blaring out our names, the prisons that we came from and the fact that whoever won the contest would be the lightweight champion of penitentiary boxing. What the voice said next was like a bucket of ice=cold water being splashed into my face, "If James 'The Machine' Manuel wins he'll set a record of being the youngest lightweight champion in the history of prison boxing!"

I walked over to the ring with my coach and trainers, climbed in and waited to be directed to the middle of the ring by the referee. The crowd was in an absolute up- roar, the bleachers were packed with a sea of black, brown, red, yellow and pale faces ... all screaming, yelling and pumping their fists in the air. They were all saying, "Rumble young man rumble!!!"

Even though I was from another institution, they all wanted me to win. There were so many emotions running around in my juvenile brain ... I felt as if I'd go crazy before I threw one punch. We walked to the middle of the ring, received our instructions from the referee and I starred up into the face of the "Assassin" his eyes were black as his

skin and the part of his eyes which were supposed to be white were blood red. He looked angry and filled with disgust. What he did next, completely caught me off guard, he puckered up his lips and kissed at me. At that moment I heard coach say, "He's gonna knock that kiss and you out cold!!!" We returned to our corners and coach asked me, "How do you beat the man?" I replied, "I beat the body!" Then the bell rang, Assassin rushed out to me and began punching. I ducked. I bobbed. I weaved and blocked but I didn't back up. I then started moving to the outside of his power hand. As I moved around the ring, I was able to keep him on the end of my jab. He caught me with a power shot to my mid-section and when I dropped my hands, he nailed me with an uppercut to my chin. I remember realizing that I'd never been hit that hard before. Strangely though, those two shots took away my nervousness. The bell rang, we stopped and returned to our corners. Coach told me to set up a double hook to his body so that I could slow him down. I nodded ok ...
The bell rang.

In round two of our scheduled 10 round light-weight title bout, I landed a stinging left hook to Assassin's side, sending him to the canvas in a delayed-reaction knockdown.

He was in obvious excruciating pain and was counted out, giving me the record setting win of my career. It was absolute pandemonium in the gym, men were running into the ring as my trainers lifted me onto their shoulders ... my ears were ringing from the loud shouts of every man in the gym. They were all yelling, "Machine! Machine! Machine!"

Chapter Seven
All That Glitters Ain't Gold

On Saturday, June 27th 1987, families from all over Virginia were gathered at Southampton Correctional Center's massive gymnasium to celebrate the scholastic and academic achievements of convicts whom had asserted themselves to achieve General Education Diplomas and College degrees.

I, by GOD'S Great Grace, was a recipient of a GED and I believed then and even now that my Mother was the proudest person in the building. My Dad and my two sisters were beaming with much pride themselves; Just knowing that I had pleased my family granted me an overwhelming sense of accomplishment.

Vonda came with my people also to witness my scholarly success. Vonda was there for me through my court trial and had helped to keep me sane, encouraged and hopeful with her affection filled letters every day of my confinement. She visited me faithfully with my kin- folk and I can say with sincere genuineness that her visits were overrunning with compassion indeed.

My admiration of her had only deepened over-time. Vonda was consistently the "WOW" factor to my heart and mind each time I saw her and every time I heard her voice. An interesting thing kept occurring during the day of my graduation. Everyone who introduced me to their families, made me known to them as "Champ James". So, I had a few grandmothers and grandfathers say to me, "Good to meet you Champ." So many people wanted me to take pictures with them and their families.

I was so humbled and honored that if my arms were long enough, I could have hugged and embraced every person in attendance. The end of the day of commencement came faster than any of us wanted but it did, unfortunately. My Mother didn't cry this time. I remember thinking that she was too happy about my graduation to cry. I hugged my relatives one by one, but when I got to Vonda something very and distinctly different happened as we approached one another. There was an anticipation of the opportunity for us to engage in a lover's embrace.

She held me close to her and her soft warm body seemed to arrest every dimension of my senses of pleasure and excitement. Her aroma was so splendidly sweet that it went into my nostrils and sojourned all the way to the deepest recesses of my heart. Then she kissed me! I desperately sought a point of reference within my memory, but I couldn't remember ever feeling like I did as her tender gesture of affection engaged my lips. Our eyes closed simultaneously and we tightened our embrace, not only did I hear a faint moan emanate from her.

I could feel the completely tantalizing vibrations of her moan. When we opened our eyes, it was if we had both awakened from a most beautiful dream. We said our goodbyes and graduation day was over.

I couldn't sleep at all that night, I kept thinking about Vonda and how much time I had left to serve on my sentence. I was so engulfed in my thoughts I was stunned to hear the guards changing shifts and it was at that time I realized I had been up all night long. Breakfast came and then Church. The inmate Pastor was a shot caller named Peter Wilson, a 47 year-old, 7'0, 285 lbs. giant (all muscle/ buff beyond belief). His knowledge of the Bible was nothing less than fascinating.

On a regular basis he would choose about ten people to randomly turn to specific scriptures of their choice and he would recite, word for word the text without flaw. Pastor Peter, could always be heard reminding the men to obey JESUS in HIS command that we "love one another."

Pastor had come to prison on an 85 year sentence when he was 22 years old for masterminding a multi-million dollar jewelry heist ring. His testimony of how he got saved was simple. He would often share the fact that he came to JESUS because he was grateful that he didn't die in a shootout with the police the day he was captured.

Church, the day after graduation was electrifying, to say the least. We all worshipped with a pure sense of gratitude and appreciation to Almighty GOD for Graciousness towards us in our endeavors in and around academia. The months left in the year zipped by and I seemed to be defending my title every other month. I came to understand fully what undisputed really meant.

By the Wonderful Grace of GOD, I never lost a fight ... all the way up to the day when I was released from my bondage, Tuesday, September 6th, 1988. Six months after my 19th birthday, Pastor Peter and several other shot callers sat in the administrations building with me as I waited for the guards to escort me out of the prison gates.

They all prayed over me and gave me words of wisdom to take with me into the free world. I was amazed by the fact that they all kept referring to me as "Champ".

Although, I was leaving a world which had trapped me behind electrified, razor wired fences, which were reinforced with towers manned by guards armed with shotguns and assault rifles. I began to shed tears of some similitude of regret. These men whom were sur- rounding me had nurtured me with such benevolent mentoring and guidance, that my journey through captivity actually accomplished molding me into a decent, morally sound and respectful man of exemplary character.

The large steel door which separated me from freedom had a ultra-thick plexiglass which I could see through to the other side where my parents, siblings and my "Boo-Thang" Vonda were waiting for me. The guards ordered the shot callers out of the room and before they left I heard one of them say, "Son remember, all that glitters ain't gold."

Chapter Eight –
Same Fight Different Round

My first step into liberty was surreal. I had dreamed of this day for years and now it was here. It wasn't a dream this time, well actually, it was a dream come true. I fell into my Mother's arms and we both cried like two big babies. Then the rest of my beloved loved ones joined us in an authentic group hug. They were in two vehicles, I jumped into my Dad's car with my Mom and Vonda. We sped off while chattering in absolute exuberance. My Dad and Vonda were informing me about how my friends were faring since their release from penitentiary two weeks before my sentence ended. I was the last one to get out, apparently there was a major mix up with my parole paperwork, my prison counselor failed to submit some essential documentation within a specified length of time, thus delaying my unfettering.
    As we drove through Richmond on our way to Creighton Court, I couldn't help but notice how drastic of a change the city had undergone since I'd left in 1983. I thought I was on another planet! When we arrived home, Vonda held on to me so tight that it was an arduous to walk from the car to the house.
    My sisters had beat us home and as I followed my parents into the house, an enormous group of people surprised me with a loud shout, "Welcome home James!"
    Everyone who had gone to prison with me was there, my aunts, uncles, cousins and neighborhood friends were there also. I could smell the scrumptious aroma of my mother's cooking and trust me ... I didn't hesitate to begin eating her food which I so missed enjoying over the years.
    For the rest of the day, I went down memory lane, was brought up to speed on many people in our community

and shared a remarkable number of laughs. There were, regrettably, some reports about how the whole city was under siege by a new drug called "crack" cocaine; the drug was so dangerous, destructive and diabolical that it was ripping away everything that we had come to know as community. Entire families were shattered beyond repair because of "crack", people were being murdered in record numbers and prisons were busting at the seams because of this substance from hell. It was in such an atmosphere that The LORD'S Most Wonderful Grace came to me in the form of a much-anticipated opportunity for me to continue my pugilistic career in a free society.

One week after my entering the public, I received a letter from Mr. Louis "Lou" Duva, who was a boxing trainer and manager who handled nineteen world champions. The Duva family promoted boxing events in over twenty countries on six continents. Some of his fighters included:

    Pernell Whitaker
    Michael Moore
    Arturo Gatti
    Meldrick Taylor
    Mark Breland
    Lennox Lewis
    Livingstone Bramble
    Mike McCallum
    Vinny Pazienza
    Hector Camacho
    …and even…
    Evander Holyfield

His office had been tracking my progress in prison and was indeed interested in bringing me under Mr. Duva's management. He noted that if I was intent on pursuing my professional vocation, I was to report within the week, to a Mr. Gerald Epperson, of "The Million Dollar Boxing Club" which was located on Richmond's south side. I knew exactly where it was and after discussing the break, shot and opportunity with my parents. I began to make preparations to follow Mr. Duva's instructions.

After months and months of vigorous training and sparring with several professionals spanning a wide range of weight classes, I finally had a chance to meet the great Lou Duva! He was an exceptionally polite and humble man whom inspired instant trust and inspiration with everyone he met. Mr. Duva's integrity was the most obvious thing about him and he spent practically the whole day breaking down all the ins and outs of professional boxing to me.

I was enthralled by the prospect of earning, at minimum, six figures for my first WBC sanctioned fight (The World Boxing Council is one of four major organizations which sanction world championship boxing bouts, along- side the International Boxing Federation, World Boxing Association and World Boxing Organization).

At the end of our meeting, Mr. Epperson turned to me and said, "James, all is well my friend, fighting in the free world is the same fight just a different round."

Two days later, my cousin, Rudolph, "Rudy" Sandford and I were on our way back to east Richmond from the boxing club. We stopped at a corner convenient store for some snacks. He purchased an orange soda and some Doritos. I picked up a Pepsi and a Snickers candy bar Rudy was one of Richmond's most feared and respected, at 23 years old, he had built an astonishing reputation as someone who was integral and genuinely trust- worthy, a powerful man of honor, no doubt, moreover, to our family he was a kind and true gentleman.

As we approached his car ... we saw someone coming towards us. I thought the guy would pass by us, but he quickly pulled out a large caliber handgun and put the barrel against my cousin's head, demanding money... then he pulled the trigger. The blast was so loud my ears were ringing. Rudy collapsed and I grabbed the guy's gun, we tussled, and the gun discharged again. This time our asailant collapsed with a shot to his forehead. I fell on my cousin and he wouldn't respond to my desperate plea for him to say something. It seemed like forever and a day before the ambulance arrived. When they reached Rudy, the attendants hooked him up to all kinds of life saving clinical and medical apparatus but when they reached the armed robber, he was pronounced DOA.

The police arrived at the same time as the ambulance and began questioning me. I explained to them what happened and one of the officers ordered me to place my hands behind my back, I complied and was cuffed; my rights were read to me, while that was happening, a small crowd had begun protesting my arrest. They were explaining to the law enforcement officers what actually took place and that I shouldn't be under arrest. The officers ignored them and rushed me to the police station. My cousin, by The Miraculous Mercy of Almighty GOD, survived his gunshot wounds. I was charged with first degree murder and denied bond; my trial took place two months later, the jury came back less than fifteen minutes later with a guilty verdict.

     And on January 19th, 1990 I was sentenced to serve 29 years in prison...

Chapter Nine –
I'll Be Just Fine, GOD'S Got Me

     The visiting room in the Richmond City Jail was completely empty when I walked in.

     I waited for my family briefly and they came through the visitor's entrance.

     It was my mom, my dad, my sisters, Vonda, my aunts, my uncles, my cousins and a few friends; Everyone was crying and completely devastated.

     I looked at them with tears in my eyes and said, "I'll be just fine, GOD'S got me."

Nathaniel Schellhase Hvizdos

ALMS FOR THE POOR

by

Nathaniel Schellhase Hvizdos

Nathaniel Schellhase Hvizdos

Alm #1

Coming to grips
Finding a path
Praise GOD
Or face wrath

Help me in
My time of stress
Somehow, I need
Out of this mess

Turn up the music
Take doctor's medicine
Help me find my way
Eventually to Heaven

Alm #2

Living infear
Living in dread
Life imbalance
Stuck in my head

Alm #3

I want to help you
I want to say
First things first
Learn to pray

Once you submit
Once you learn
Look for the best
At every turn

Your mind starts to clear
Your soul shines true
This the first step
This first step for you

Alm #4

Once you have faith
Once you have grown
Truth of life
Becomes known

After all is seen
Blind must see
Beyond your walls
You become free

Possessions are yours
Obtain what you need
Yet live your life
Free from all greed

Plant your garden
Water to nourish
Dirt now green
Watch it flourish

Alm #5

Ask for forgiveness
Ask for peace
Be coherent
Find release

Set a new path
Find a new way
For your direction
Must daily pray

Enjoy the Sun
Enjoy the Moon
Keep your heart warm
Help yourself bloom

And with fine food
Nourish your soul
Drink your water
Pay your full toll

If you have trouble
If life is dark
Search in yourself
Seek out a spark

Pull up your blanket
Rest now your head
Seek happiness
Among all the dread

Alm #6

Look to the sky
Look to the Earth
Find now purpose
For your own birth

Make connections
Look for signs
Amidst the rivers
Amidst mountain pines

Have fear when needed
Be brave above all
Believe in yourself
Even when you fall

Alm #7

Your thoughts are many
Your soul is one
Sleep at night
Rise with the Sun

Follow your heart
Remember to smile
Realize your dreams
Within each mile

Seek out guidance
See bad and good
Ask for forgiveness
Know yes you should

No one is perfect
All can grow wise
Work towards goals
No matter the size

To get where you want
Reverence a must
Cleanse with reflection
Pray for GOD's trust

It may take a month
It may take years
Rejoice as you go
There will be tears

Alm #8

In all you do
Seek to repent
Enter with care
Be Heaven sent

Reach out to others
Share light with them
Do not be a sham
Shine like a gem

When you see hurt
Do not look away
Offer your hand
Together you pray

Cold chills come
Heat also burns
Those who relate
Everyone learns

As the Earth turns
Abundance enthralls
Be not afraid
Forgiveness calls

Alm #9

Seek to understand
Seek to know
Helping others
You shall grow

Plant a seed
Incarnation
Can you aide
Satiation

In your time
Spread your love
Warming feeling
Like a glove

Do not see the end
See a beginning
Following light
See yourself winning

Have a vision
Make it come true
All you need
Resides in you

Alm #10

What reason am I here?
Please why am I alive
Surely to help others
To help others thrive

Once you have done this
After you awake
Problems seem fixable
Hearts you won't break

Instead must seek solutions
Service above self
Life will have more meaning
Like books upon a shelf

And like the Moon and Sun
You will light a way
With every problem won
Remember thanks and pray

Alm #11

Now that you are thinking
You are just getting started
Weight upon your back
You have always carted

Breathe deep in love
Breathe out all pain
Accept who you are
Live not in vain

Love yourself strong
Give self permission
Then basketball scores
You will be swishin'

Your mission you seek
Acceptance a must
Love yourself first
Learn how to trust

Sharpen your thoughts
Clarity beams
Embrace eternity
Enact your dreams

Alm #12

Sure you have faults
Yes you have flaws
Accept yourself
Reflect and pause

Now you want change
Make yourself better
Warmth from the cold
Like that of a sweater

Wrap yourself up
In life as you know it
Make every effort
To others you show it

Offer up thanks
Ask for forgiveness
Lead like a tiger
How you must live this

Allow to be healed
Try to heal others
We are all born
Of earthly mothers

And into tomorrow
Looking around
Life will be better
See how you sound

Listen intently
Share what you learn
Slowly but surely
No longer to burn

Alm #13

Your dialogue has started
Within your own mind
Take a long moment
What did you find

An inkling here
Reflection there
Introspection
Now more aware

It is just a start
And where you will go
Somewhere for sure
In time you will know

Take now each step
With care and love
Bow down your head
To GOD above

And as you run
Slow down to walk
Listen attentive
To how people talk

**Lift up your chin
Be ever alert
Help one another
Healing their hurt**

**And as you go
Must also follow
Looking at you
No longer hollow**

Alm #14

Brush off your shoulders
Find your own tune
Introspection the key
Morning night noon

As you find answers
Your key fits the lock
Music enlightens
Solid as a rock

As the clock turns
Minutes go by
You're not alone
Help others fly

Swallow your pride
Don't be too loud
Observe time go by
Don't be too proud

In time you will find
Answers inside
Spread wide your wings
Learn to confide

Alm #15

You seek to change
Regrets you have
Time to sacrifice
But not a calf

Feel your pockets
Share your wealth
Anonymously
Without self

Do not keep count
Do not ask why
See injustice
See people cry

Maybe it's you
You will not lose
Choices made daily
Yes you must choose

Bow down to GOD
Submit your will
Reach out your plate
For GOD to fill

Food of the soul
Finding in prayer
Making contact
Please do not scare

When time is right
Actions are blessed
Seeing all love
Above the mess

Distress all around
This planet amazing
At GOD's table
We all are grazing

Alm #16

Inspect how you are
Instead of how it is
Remember where you're from
Instead of media biz

You're somehow detained
Now walking the line
A new golden land
Someday you will find

Instead of insane
Try to be renewed
Like each cup of coffee
That's slowly brewed

Remember where you're at
Remember to change
Slowly you must crawl
Psyche rearrange

Alm #17

Have you not yet
Learned how to smile
Has it now been
A little while

For what reason
Why do you frown
Are you really
A monster of town

Likely you're not
And I can bet
Your eyes before
Have become wet

Wet from tears
Wet from grief
Renew daily
Spirit belief

Ask forgiveness
Forgive yourself
Life is such chaos
Disorganized shelf

Take each product
That you need
Apply generously
Where you bleed

Give it time
Healing is slow
And as you heal
You start to grow

Within your thoughts
Seek alignment
Light of Heaven
Your assignment

Shine on others
As you learn
Good and bad
You shall discern

Time to awake
Beyond your faults
Ablution ensues
All your pain halts

Alm #18

Do not forget
Or falter to follow
Become whole
Fill your hollow

Torch lights guide
Lead on a horse
For gun and sword
Have full remorse

Cold dead nights
Be now gone
Onward troops
Focus game on

Onward you go
Marching headlong
Into your battle
Right against wrong

To die or to live
Our bright flag waves
You are alive
Avoided mass graves

While Generals watch
From distant hills
Valorous roles
Healing bleak wills

You made it through
Now must question
Were you all wrong
Learning your lesson

Alm #19

Look to the sky
Look to the Earth
Look to your death
Look to your birth

Find a question
Find an answer
Be a singer
Be a dancer

Write your story
Draw your art
Pile it all
In a cart

Push your cart
Make your point
Let it pour
From every joint

If you can
You will see
Captive soul
Now set free

If you can
Share your worth
Reflect on death
Reflect on birth

Alm #20

Are you tormented
Are you vulnerable
Must be tolerant
Must be venerable

Holy practice
Spiritual ways
Remember thanks
Remember praise

Alm #21

Confusion overwhelms
Darkness is close
Lift yourself strong
To yourself toast

Remember your past
Not self-deprecation
Testing is a lesson
Practicing-deflation

Have accomplishments
You are a human
Perfection is not real
Creation is now bloomin'

Reflect in the mirror
Gaze but don't cry
Give yourself wings
In time you shall fly

Sprout from a seed
Share what you've given
Crawl to your feet
A mission you're livin'

As the leaves fall
In winter stay warm
Reconciliation
Weather life's storm

Alm #22

Do you always feel
Like you're falling down
A bit of feces
Upon the ground

Well give it a flush
Look at your cards
Life can be dismal
Life can be hard

And as you spin
Head in the dark
Look now again
For a new spark

Kindle that glow
Observe and view
Something golden
Can happen for you

Do not give up
Do not give in
There is great hope
Beyond all this din

Alm #23

If you're alone
Lost and distraught
Angry with yourself
Over people you fought

Raise yourself up
Learn what you've done
Mistakes and lessons
Allow yourself sun

Feel day upon you
Rise and shine new
Give yourself a break
Try not to feel blue

We've all hurt people
We all have regrets
Trying to do better
To recount our debts

Introspection to find
A better side of you
Life is not a movie
This my friend true

Imperfect human acts
Committed every day
You're your own keeper
Wake up now and pray

Alm #24

Love above hate
Joy above pain
Hope above despair
Life lives from rain

Allow water to nourish
A tender shared embrace
Set your sights beyond
Our common daily race

If you seek forgiveness
If you seek release
Realize imperfection
That you're not a beast

Instead you're a flower
Initial budding bloom
Supersonic healing
Supersonic boom

Time starts to wander
Minutes slip past steady
Is your soul improving
Steadfast are you ready

Alm #25

Looking outside
River ocean lake
Always must be real
Never again be fake

Take a walk to the water
Let the feeling cleanse
Offer respect to GOD
See beyond all ends

Learn all from inside
Illuminate your soul
Learn from mistakes
Climb out of your hole

Relate to life anew
Take a breath of light
Regret some actions past
You can feel more right

As you sleep and wake
See the signs abound
Realize you are free
Listen how you sound

Alm #26

When midnight screams
Silent bad dreams
Panic feeling like
Gone moonlight beams

No light for me
All painful thoughts
Alone under covers
My happiness rots

So I pull on my hat
And crawl in a hole
And as I suffer
Life takes its toll

Alone in this world
With no one who cares
No one to listen
People's blank stares

Not on any teams
To relate to me
Bound in a cage
Supposedly free

If I had dreams
That gave me peace
Somehow it seems
Would be my release

Nothing to say
Time now to pray
Fallen again
I've lost my way

And then there is light
That voice from beyond
Giving me guidance
Strong spiritual bond

Then to the sky
And to inside
Focused again
Positive ride

Alm #27

Dusty gravel thoughts
Self-deprecation
Dry diluted water
Self-mutilation

Engulfed in confusion
Words steal my happy
On my knees ego
Feeling quite crappy

Bullet execution
Weight of divinity
Feeling tomorrows
Thoughts of infinity

Can I not help myself
Is GOD not around
Meditation on love
I start to rebound

Imprisoned again
But I have the key
Repent with intent
Forgive peacefully

Alm #28

Lost feeling insane
As I rise broken
Words that are silent
Definitely spoken

Actions are louder
Make now with haste
Sick and in pain
I think I'm waste

Stares that can gouge
Glass also cuts
We have all been
Stuck in life's ruts

I am soot sore
Living in dread
Kneel to GOD's throne
Calm now my head

I can look up
Stretch to the Moon
Remembering joy
A child's balloon

Alm #29

Okay let us talk
Skin color issue
Makes me so sad
I need a tissue

Police can kill
And not face time
No punishment
To fit their crime

Black lives matter
As all lives do
See in the media
These videos true

Body cameras off
But others record
Our justice system
I am abhorred

Think now again
At what you have seen
And all charges dropped
What does that mean

Yet still the clock turns
As the calendar goes
We are all brothers
And they are our foes

Racism rampant
In our USA
Vote with your conscience
Remember to pray

Alm #30

If you have rejected GOD
And welcomed the devil
Immediately time
To get on the level

Pray every day
Must reject all evil
Prepare yourself
Swift mental upheaval

This journey is rough
But it must be done
Before you revealed
Faith in the ONE

As time unfolds
You will start sailing
Goodness will come
After some wailing

I scream faith to you
You must scream it too
Not at first loud
But silent and true

Thoughts will come in
Mixed good and bad
Seek self-forgiveness
Accept you are sad

As your soul levels
Sun will shine in
Weather will calm
Soon you shall grin

Yes judge yourself
Learn from your past
Daily repentance
Until the last

Give it some time
There is no quick fix
And as you reflect
Still the clock ticks

Give yourself faith
Seek out the good
Put out your fire
Accept that you should

Alm #31

GOD welcomes you
To the table of life
Answers your prayers
A way out of strife

Follow your gut
Have good intent
Listen to learn
End blind consent

If your goal is to heal
You shall be fed
If your goal is to rule
You will live in dread

Somehow you relate
Positive food
Be present to heal
Try not to be rude

Check yourself daily
Make yourself humble
It's a tough climb
Yes we all stumble

Brush yourself off
Learn from mistakes
Learn from success
Cause no more heartbreaks

As time progresses
Gold treasure you find
Perhaps not cash money
There's more than one kind

Alm #32

Speak to the universe
Offer daily thanks
End subversion
End all your pranks

Follow the way
Revolve around prayer
Meditate on life
Anytime everywhere

Look to the world
Seek community
Take yourself out
Work for unity

Water food sun and sleep
Ask for daily blessings
Eat healthy meals and share
Feel yourself progressing

Make pleasing others key
Accountable to self
Have no excuses
Always offer help

As you engage others
Enacting altruism
Don't ever destroy
Light that is within them

Instead be a conduit
From now only good deeds
A soul that's satisfied
Is a soul that reads

Alm #33

If you feel that no one cares
Within yourself understand
Earth is full of chaos
Isn't what you've planned

Tie your shoes daily
Eat at least one meal
Be aware of yourself
Until you stand to feel

Worth of others crucial
Value your own life
End dependence quickly
Alleviate your strife

Go out and about
Find will to improve
Concepts will reveal
Own your personal groove

Do not give up yet
Do not just cave in
Your life can get better
Make efforts to win

Set goals for tomorrow
Striving to achieve
Don't always be dark
In yourself believe

A spiritual path
Is what you need
Don't live life to die
Never service greed

Alm #34

So you have attitude
Check it at the door
So you have anger
Have anger no more

You should seek answers
Be part of a solution
Figure out yourself
Find personal ablution

Sinister thoughts no more
Acts of kindness yes
Issues of society
Help clean up this mess

Strive to excel and find
Ways to soothe your pain
Leave negativity behind
So much yet still to gain

When you've made a step
Do you leave a wake
Is your trail pure
Others don't forsake

Explore a life of joy
End existing hate
Slowly and securely
Alignment to your fate

Try to change your spirit
Consciously you tread
Pray to GOD each day
Clearing out your head

Alm #35

Darkness enwraps your soul
Pray for the Light of GOD
Allow forgiveness to yourself
Hear your Angels applaud

You have done some good
You have much more to do
Don't self-relish with praise
Instead to GOD be true

Who are you here to help
What enlightenment is there
Who among the masses
What burdens do they bare?

Can you offer assistance
Offer a helping hand
Your plan yet unknown
Yet know that it is grand

This world rough and rocky
Become a beacon of light
Helping all downtrodden
Help them feel right

Alm #36

You are to be a bird
First locked in an egg
Soon to see sunlight
Have patience now I beg

Pecking free a hole
Now time is ready
Look at yourself now
Free though unsteady

Feathers to form
Be nurtured first
Parental assurance
Feeding your thirst

Soon you have feathers
Spreading your wings
Growing quite quickly
Your parent sings

Tweet tweet tweet
Learn now your song
Flutter your feathers
Survival not wrong

Jump from the nest
Make your first flight
Yes you can do it
It will feel right

Still to the nest
Everyday return
Until self-sufficient
Feel yearning burn

Next on your own
Build your own nest
Life is beginning
Remember to rest

Alm #37

I am but a speck
Not worth a penny
Is this how you feel
Then you feel plenty

Time to turn it around
Give yourself a break
Realize time is abundant
Picture you as a cake

Sweet and tasty
A treat to most
Cheers to yourself
Have yourself a toast

Alm #38

So what's up
You are in the dumps
So cheer up
Awake your heart pumps

It isn't over yet
You have time to change
Master your thoughts
Mentally rearrange

Cheer yourself up
Thank GOD anew
Every day now
Thankful and true

Lift up your spirit
Polish your shoes
Nourish your wounds
Heal every bruise

Now pick a shirt
Make sure it's clean
Take yourself out
And stop being mean

Forgive your past deeds
Learn don't forget
Tomorrow shines light
Pay back your debt

Alm #39

Shabby and rusty
Your energy low
Forgiveness from GOD
Possible to know

If you repent
Make daily prayer
Life will rebound
You can get there

Time does not matter
There's plenty for you
Weeks months years
You must stay true

You can hide from others
But not from yourself
And GOD ever-present
Don't think you are stealth

Into tomorrow go
With love in your heart
Feel free creatively
Now wake up to art

Use self-expression
Don't steal lie kill
Stand at the gates
Control your own will

Alm #40

Give yourself courage
Find inner strength
Forgive your misdoings
See infinite length

Infinity abounds
Heaven calling all
Pick yourself up
Up from your fall

Forgiveness is free
Time we say heals
Peace can be yours
Feel how it feels

Find tattered ways
Raise a new flag
Give frequent praise
Let your tail wag

Conjure up love
Give it up to others
And love yourself
Have warmth for another

Alm #41

You've done your time
You've paid your price
Now treat yourself
To something nice

Life is hard
It's been better
Buy a new shirt
Perhaps a new sweater

You have nothing
But you are free
How about ice cream
Maybe a CD

Clear your soul
Find now a job
No longer can you
Lie steal and mob

Clear your soul
Free your thoughts
Forgive yourself
Forming new plots

Define a plan
Then write it down
Cherish love
Change your frown

If you can
Reveal all truth
Be for real
Don't be aloof

Kiss the sky
Heal your soul
Soon you will see
Life anew whole

Have a heart
Be more caring
Develop hope
That's more daring

Alm #42

You've squandered your days
Lost in a maze
To find your way out
Offer up praise

Give of yourself
Volunteer time
Penance a must
Made for your crime

Some call it sin
That led to remorse
Be now for good
Change your soul's course

Live now for light
Shun away dark
Dismal soggy days
Need but a spark

Find in your heart
A need in your life
Cut away anger
As if with a knife

Trim off the pain
Clean out your wound
Forgiveness is now
You will heal soon

Time is your doctor
Friendship shall come
What is your debt
Pay back the sum

Sprout angel wings
Learn to share joy
As if a child
Who plays with a toy

Reflect on your past
It has not been great
Your appointment is now
Do not be late

Alm #43

Crumple not your soul
Don't throw it in the trash
Find the good in life
And keep it in a stash

Add to it each day
Smile at another
Piling up the joy
Give it to the other

Victory is love
Work for it each day
Someday it will come
Awaken now to pray

Enjoy skies of peace
Forgiveness gives you strength
Sacred spirit release
Share it to any length

Solitude must go
Community embrace
Synchronistic flow
Developing your pace

Life is not defined
Time becomes a friend
Flourishing with water
Nourished to ascend

Alm #44

Seek out fresh air
Breathe free in light
This is a beginning
Use Love to fight

Fight now for good
See feathers form
Strengthening your neck
Free from the storm

Flight will be yours
Once you grow strong
Wings you shall flap
Do no more wrong

Accept help from others
Let yourself grow
Patience my friend
Time you must sew

Out of the nest
Chirp chirp squawk squawk
Rise to your feet
First try to walk

See all around you
Blue sky and sun
Gather your thoughts
Seek to be one

One with yourself
Ability grows
Practice and stretch
Head to your toes

Then when you tickle
And feel time to try
Hop from the nest
It's your turn to fly

Alm #45

Exercise daily
Body and thoughts
Be like a sailor
Learn to tie knots

Upon waves in ocean
Balance your walk
Ship jostles slowly
So does your talk

People see through you
Know you can't fool
Words be your anchor
In the World pool

Once you were reckless
Caused hurricanes
Jeopardized others
For personal gains

As for tomorrow
As for next year
Spread only clarity
Cause no more fear

Give others joy
Sail to calm water
Follow the stars
No longer slaughter

Bring forth the cargo
Safely to port
Fulfill your mission
Do not abort

See new horizons
Set sail to win
Spiritual guidance
From inside begin

Alm #46

Life is a marathon
Long is the path
First you must practice
Years do the math

Stretch and condition
Strength and endurance
Others will teach you
Learn from assurance

First you feel pain
Heart beating fast
Sweating profusely
Unsure if you'll last

First it's a mile
Walking to run
Be steadfast
Try to have fun

First get good shoes
A shirt and a tie
Hydrate your system
See your heart fly

Feeling too crazy
Dripping out sweat
Agony fills you
Things you regret

Yet over time
Stamina improves
Developing muscles
Evolving your moves

As you will find
This journey fulfills
And when you succeed
Find warmth replace chills

Alm #47

Lay right down
And close your eyes
Seeking to find
Your mortal prize

Seeing yourself
Yet to be born
What will you do
On your first morn'

What are your hopes
Goals to achieve
Values upheld
What to believe

A baby new
Brought into life
Can you yet see
Overcome strife

And do you see
Goals upon high
Things you should do
Before you die

Is it for wealth
Or seeing to heal
A polished coin
How do you feel

To be wanted
Lost Mom and Dad
To cheer others
When they are sad

A reverent life
Or one of din
It is now time
Time to begin

Set yourself goals
And follow through
Forgive yourself
To GOD be true

Alm #48

You are an old leaf
Fallen to forest floor
Rotting and decaying
Like an old apple core

Unbeknownst to you
Cycle is unending
Renewed through rebirth
Now naturally mending

Time lights anew
Spirit again grows
Caught in between
Amidst all the throws

Do not give up yet
Nutrients you are
Set sights on mending
Set your sights far

As the farmers turn soil
You're part of growth again
Seeking inner peace
Be middle path Zen

Sunshine water power
Reaching for the sky
Become a new beginning
To live again try

As you grow to learn
Life returns to you
Forgiven not forgotten
Freedom yes it's true

Alm #49

Inspired by bright lightning
Captured in a rain
Memories of life forming
Returned again to pain

What you've done to others
What they've done to you
Lights camera action
Imprisonment in blue

Can't you see what's happening
Mad circles of your mind
Blood and trouble swirling
Entangled in a bind

Stuck within a room
The door you cannot open
Windows boarded shut
Forgotten gone no hopin'

As you starved and dry
Stomach pains ignite
Hiding all the time
Let in a little light

Soon these walls will crumble
When you're on your knees
Pray to GOD for help
Ask for summer breeze

Look aloft to see
An eagle is above
Offer up your thanks
Learn to accept love

When the time is right
Only you will know
Return to sound and sight
Let positivity flow

Alm #50

Enough with my lecture
Enough with conjecture
Organized words
About improving texture

Words about praise
One GOD above
No time for hate
All time for love

Seek time to listen
Find time to pray
Keep your composure
Each night and each day

Do not recite
Ills of your past
Connection a must
Friendship to last

Enjoy conversations
Laugh smile eat
Offer yourself
In cold or in heat

As you reach out
And gain other's trust
Money will come
Sadness will bust

Dream the big dreams
Non-violently fight
You must believe
Success is your right

Alm #51

Falling falling falling
Through an empty sky
You're a drop of water
Perhaps about to die

Then a plant catches you
You trickle to its root
Refreshed in attitude
Transgressions now moot

Into the plant you go
Into sun so bright
Luminescent green
Butterflies alight

Nourishment as food
Moisture fight to live
What more can be asked
To give and give and give

Alm #52

From you to me
I'm a choking victim
Suffocating slowly
Lost within our system

If I could breathe
Yes I would survive
Now I guess I can
Because I'm still alive

Breath however not steady
Grasping hard for gulps
Struggling from mistakes
Lost in all my hopes

And so along I tread
Trying hard to swim
Cement shoes on my feet
My future looming dim

Yet look to the horizon
Light beacon now shining
Pointless seems my crying
And fruitless my whining

See into tomorrow
Breathing more secure
I have a new task
I have a new chore

See the best in others
See no one as small
Straightening my back
Answering the call

Alm #53

I am angry
I am mad
I'm confused
I am sad

Never knew my mom
Never knew my dad
Life's never been good
It's always been bad

Born at the bottom
Opportunities none
Seems all I have
Fast food and sun

I feel crippled
With no one to care
Seeing my posture
My animal stare

Public assistance
Delinquent kid
Blown my top
I've blown my lid

Life is dismal
Future grim
Can you see
No too dim

Alm #54

Crushed by fate
Feeling low
I am caught
Undertow

I need your help
I need some love
Human to human
Not from above

My spirit is cut
Morale all lost
Without anyone
Can't pay the cost

Bills overdue
Eviction is here
Feeling alone
Devil is near

And so I fold
Give up the game
Time to erupt
Let loose my pain

Punching kicking stealing
Robbing my neighbor
Hurting and hating
My negative labor

Then comes a hand
May it redeem
I pray now to GOD
Selecting my team

Alm #55

I feel like I'm magic
Feeling like I now care
Like Pink Floyd says
Is there anybody out there

Been walking for years
No one to talk to
Isolated in public
Alone I walk through

In my abyss
My pain grows strong
What a malfunction
Where is my song

When all along
Chains invisible
Does anyone care
I am miserable

To forgive myself
I pray to the sky
Asking for answers
Questioning why

Then shackles broken
I feel a small glow
No longer in line
In life's death row

It seems I can smile
Though my teeth frown
I am now an eagle
I Fly all around

This choice I have made
To seek out another
And in the quickness
Earth now my mother

And to her I cling
Nurtured and loved
No longer a problem
Winter hands gloved

And as I warm to her
My fate not yet sealed
Thanks be to others
I feel I am healed

Alm #56

I and I one
Together we band
Brethren of life
As much as is sand

Tickled by waves
Fish all around
Swimming above us
Almost silent sound

Seagulls cavort
Dolphins here play
Oceans of existence
Together we pray

Thankful to GOD
Blessed in the light
No longer dreading
Things that aren't right

Chuckling yes
Aloud now to laugh
We have enlightened
Our middle path

Tickled by inklings
Subtle and joyous
Little life's burdens
Cannot annoy us

And as we enjoy
Time here on Earth
Solace and comfort
We find our rebirth

Kissed on the forehead
Told we are good
Reverent to all
Just like we should

Alm #57

I've had let downs frowns
Many breakdowns drowns
Saddened by life stories
Been around many towns

Had a car to mobilize
Couple dollars table chairs
Awoke cut and bruised
Blacked out public glares

Drunk and deranged
Lost years caused tears
Memories umknown
Payback in the gears

Then in the mirrors
Clearing my mind
Seeing myself
Only to find

Hatred of self
Respect level zero
Failed my mentors
Failed by heroes

Soon enough thoughts
Silent in knots
Next thing I know
Sleeping on cots

Mixed in the mix
Homeless shelf life
Realized the bottom
Facing GOD's knife

Then to the clock
Calendar time
See people caring
Beyond personal crime

Alm #58

I've been like leather
Brittle cracked torn
Sun bleached and wrinkled
Definitely worn

I was not thrown away
Or burned in a fire
Or cut-up repurposed
Somehow had desire

Add conditioning oil
Made supple with wax
Polished once again
Taken to the max

Definitely not new
Yet somehow cherished
Pride now returning
Proud not embarrassed

From I and I
Crossed the bridge together
Sometimes was a flood
Often sunny weather

Alm #59

I am a musician
I am the music
Beats see me through
Determine my rubric

It solves my problems
Turns off my frown
Evolving from sadness
Forgiven as clown

Midnight revelations
Repeat 3am solitude
Accompanied by beats
Positive attitude

You are me
I am you
Together we shine
No longer blue

With melodies saving
Back from the edge
Walking inline
Taming the hedge

Nathaniel Schellhase Hvizdos

So we clip on
Songs of my soul
Found a new road
Paid the good toll

<u>Alm #60</u>

I did not know
Life could improve
I was always running
Lost on the move

Couldn't take silence
Could not reflect
I became sober
With no self-respect

In moderation
Solemn regret
Damned forever
My only bet

Then came a notion
Like AC in summer
Prayed for redemption
Got off my bummer

Realized a future
Could be worth my time
With GOD in the picture
I turned on a dime

Then to the books
I started to read
Masters of words
Taught me to breathe

I broke from the old
Came clean in thoughts
Began to see light
Untying life's knots

Alm #61

I am a messenger
Actions and words
History and trees
Bees and songbirds

I am not alone
Yet no one is here
In suffering times
Lost amidst fear

Sometime tomorrow
Or just now it passed
Heaven is with me
Praise to the last

No longer crying
Or angered to rage
Free on the Earth
To turn this page

I can read or not
Or sleep with a smile
Paying my penance
Been through a trial

As my heart cramps
Pain I now feel
Knowing another
Keeps my script real

Passive to some
Persistent when needed
GOD's love guides
Directions I've heeded

And as for now
Feel motivation
Help one another
Transform a nation

Alm #62

I'm nothing but a scrub
Filth of the Earth
Low down decrepit
No value no worth

Can you not see
Raised to be scum
Never had a thing
Known only to bum

I hold my sign
Side of the road
Needing some bucks
Life as a toad

From shadows I hop
Ask you to give
Humanities scourge
This how I live

A dollar or two
Burger smoke drink
Charity love
You care I think

With your spare change
I live in woods
Intoxicated camp
A life among hoods

Somehow some way
Now have new shoes
Somehow a job
Incredible news

Yeah I got up
Accepted a home
No longer forgotten
No longer to roam

Believe it or not
Battlefield won
Because of blind love
I now see the sun

Thank you to GOD
Prayer found a way
Brought me to life
Now it's my day

Alm #63

GOD put me here
To take away fear
To face my fear
To heal my fear

Platinum day alive
Finding a new hope
Warrior of love
Strengthening to cope

Do not retreat
Do not withdraw
Engaging problems
Mending each flaw

Follow the good
Lose not your light
Keep now your cool
Do only right

Let past be gone
Future your grace
Light your new hearth
Make smile your face

Use words of joy
Recite self-repair
See what you win
Sit in a chair

Pray think and renew
Feel your legs steady
Stand up more proud
When you are ready

Alm #64

I am drunk
I'm depressed
From what I see
Life is all messed

Chaotic energy
Just like a fire
I am all done
Worn like a tire

My thoughts .
Are unclear
And clear
Blurry smear

Cannot think
Another drink
From the store
I am a stink

Can you see
My sweet fear
Aura in headlights
Just like a deer

Flora and fauna
Hop filled cup
Stuck in a zone
All zipped up

Like in a bag
Quick suffocation
Cannot breathe
No more elation

Lost me
In a funk
Once again
I am drunk

Then I sleep
Out many hours
Dreaming of life
Finding life's flowers

I remember
Time away
Sleep to clear
Awake I pray

Vision from
Midnight thought
Now I am here
Am here to plot

Plot a new me
I need support
My salvation
Hope to purport

And in an instant
I am saved
Holy for life
Until my grave

Alm #65

Yesterday was not my day
My prayer to make anew
Tomorrow will be my crop
Hope and aspirations grew

Now I know I want change
Breaking rules my old game
Extend myself to new heights
Take away sad stain my name

Understand my past
Best of me not shown
Please judge my future
See my goodness grown

Before was a frown with a glare
Stared people down everywhere
Here I am now learning love
Trying to show people I care

I know now I can mend
Forgave myself old ways
Unity my goal today
A man who offers praise

Alm #66

I love GOD anew
And now I pray always
Arisen from below
Rescind learned ghetto ways

No ills to please
No fear to spread
GOD my savior
Beyond when I'm dead

Light and abundance
Joy and laughter
Friendship with others
That's what I'm after

Been tempted before
Walked spreading hate
I've found forgiveness
It is never too late

You can do this too
Just open your door
Salvation is free
Don't have to be poor

Find riches of soul
Gold in your prayer
Wherever you are
It is right there

Available to all
Those willing to love
Seek all your answers
From One GOD above

Alm #67

Tender mercy
Be mine please
Been a long while
Since I felt a breeze

Sweltering hotness
Dripping in sweat
Caves filled with fire
Forever in debt

The boss of my hood
Kept my noose tight
Forced to serve evil
I knew it wasn't right

So sad and so down
Could see no way out
Destined for prison
In shackles I shout

Settled for less
Got served my time
Life among lifers
Locked up for crime

Yet soon I'll be free
And what do I see
Nine years later
I found the key

To better myself
I split from the crowd
Studied and learned
Polished and proud

Made a new turn
Broke from my past
Returning citizen
At last yes at last

Once I am out
I will get a job
No longer poised
To drug rape and rob

I'll pray for myself
Work as I must
Prove to others
In me they can trust

And when I succeed
Then One GOD will show
Ready for Heaven
To fly and to glow

Alm #68

I was born wealthy
Once gave none to others
Cadillac lifestyle
No love for my brothers

Yet as I have grown
Friends became few
On the side of the road
I turn now to you

Sign says GOD bless
Homeless please help
I pass on some dollars
To quiet their yelp

It makes me feel good
To help those in need
I've mended my ways
Can't prosper with greed

Alm #69

I've never liked medicine
Would never take pills
But my doctor now says
I suffer some ills

Take these couple things
Morning noon and night
Come back in two months
To see if they're right

Now pay as you go
Pharmacy time
You will feel better
With each clock chime

Remember to schedule
Your next appointment
I am very busy
And oh here's some ointment

Toodles for now
Be good to yourself
Then the doc's gone
Notes on his shelf

This cannot be
I feel really down
Should have stayed home
Skipped doctor town

Friends and family agree
Gave medicine its due
Try prescription pills
They're there to help you

In prayer I look up
Asking now why
If I don't take these
I may as well die

And if you comply
Listen to doctors
Blindly take pills
Before bedtime covers

In time they may help
You learn a new way
Science mysterious
That's all I can say

Then if you soon find
Your health brings you down
Trust in another
To turn you around

Alm #70

My pain is too much
Suffering my soul
I have surely fallen
Life's taken its toll

This world so cruel
Many suffer alone
With no sense of home
A course grinding stone

In a pit I lay
Broken and injured
And now to this day
Much pain I endured

How to get out
How to revive
To dream again
Thrive and survive

Who can help me
Who is out aware
Answer for all
Meditative prayer

And I push on
Trying to find
Forgiven soul
New peace of mind

Alm #71

Some things are big
Much to overcome
Forget that notion
Find a new drum

Follow the beat
Escape the heat
Set your own pace
And move your feet

See ahead struggles
Valley to mountain
Fresh water awaits
Pristine spring fountain

Take in the air
Sip given water
Feel life renewed
Free from the slaughter

If you can make it
Yes you will see
What was a seed
Is now a tree

Alm #72

Two drops of rain
Rivers overflowing
Two drops of pain
Anxiety growing

Oceans of sadness
We can do this together
Find higher ground
Above all bad weather

I am now sure
GOD loves me too
Prayer answers all
Questions ensue

Hercules strength
Wisdom of Buddha
Guaranteed winner
Peace barracuda

My mind is rowing
Direction I choose
Flood is upon us
Stars give me clues

And to those who doubt
Say save it for later
My sunshine is out
Don't ever be a hater

Alm #73

I am in love
With a day called tomorrow
More time on Earth
Must ask now to borrow

These years I now need
To set and meet goals
I've been lost awhile
Need to fill a few holes

Songs yet to write
Joy yet to hear
Days to unshackle
Bring others cheer

Too much to cover
Must have more time
With GOD as my wind
My music will chime

Alm #74

Been feeling unsafe
Been feeling unkind
Been told I'm uptight
I need to unwind

I've considered the knife
I've thought of the gun
Suicide by pills
My life is no fun

My sleeping is bad
My wake time is worse
Everything sucks
Alive in a curse

Yet a hand reached out
And added some words
Speaking new things
Things I've not heard

Chills now are going
Starting to warm
Thankful for love
Amidst my own storm

This hurricane calming
Weather less rough
With help from others
My life is less tough

Now I am hoping
Not choking and grey
Stoking GOD's fire
Awake now I pray

And with this new mind
Life has more light
Suffocating no more
Things seem alright

Alm #75

We wrestled
We lost
We paid
The cost

Been broken
And beaten
Been cut up
And eaten

Now we are feces
Flushed and forgotten
Societal sewage
Downtrodden rotten

Fumes are ghastly
Our souls but ghosts
Vacant composure
Darkness our hosts

Yet somehow
Some way
Some where
Today

Nathaniel Schellhase Hvizdos

I stand up
You should too
Must look up
Find new glue

Get back together
Find a new form
Straighten your spine
Back to the norm

Yes I can do it
Yes you can too
Increasing pride
Ponder this clue

That which is first
Had once been last
Planning next steps
Life going fast

Set now a plan
Next follow through
Once was a sprout
With water it grew

And like a plant
Sunshine we reach
Teachers help you
Practice and preach

Nathaniel Schellhase Hvizdos

Success with time
Prepared not to fail
Each boat different
Each boat will sail

Alm #76

Roller coaster
Alcohol
Feeling big
Feeling small

First I am grand
Then I am weak
Mentality gone
All hide and seek

If I am down
It seems to help
But now I know
I've lost myself

Liquor store buzz
Sell sell sell sell
An easy ticket
To living hell

Phone is ringing
Who would call
Imagination
No one at all

So here I stand
Ready to change
Self-realization
Must rearrange

On a new path
Freedom from ill
Finding slowly
My own free will

Can you smile
Smile at me
I need some love
Cannot you see

Suffering less
Joy in each day
Focus again
Awake I pray

Alm #77

Belief in unseen
My death I ponder
Still forge ahead
Way up yonder

How can I be
A better soul
Emergence from
My personal hole

Vacant blank stares
Empty of thought
Nothing is good
Here where I rot

I look ahead
Focus on light
Find my vision
Awaking from night

Demons can lurk
Actions were bad
Please forgive me
GOD I am sad

Done harm too much
Did others low
Please teach me how
How to please grow

Up with the sun
Awaken and live
Teach me please GOD
Teach how to give

Alm #78

I am a slice
Of green pepper
Crispy and tasty
Dancing stepper

Sharing my moves
Grooving along
Changing my tune
In my own song

Once was raucous
Rude crude and mean
Now I whistle
Nice fresh and clean

Washing my clothes
Brushing my chops
Friend to many
Life never stops

Sharing my joy
Please come along
Spread all my wealth
Gained from my song

Rich with pure water
Nourishing well
Be of the ONE
Love show and tell

Wishing for love
Far near and wide
Shining it forth
Peace from inside

Be now correct
Never know wrong
Enjoying life
This is our song

Alm #79

In the food
Where we mix
At the table
Get our licks

In my stomach
Food it blends
Satiation
On the mends

Get your fill
Find a calm
Live your life
Like a psalm

Savor herbs
Food and drink
At the table
Where we think

Afterwards
Pray and rest
Peacefully
At your best

Lick your lips
Napkin clean
Palate quenched
Mental glean

Alm #80

I want to help
Not to hamper
I want to shine
Not be a damper

Once a camper
Built the fire
Enjoyed chaos
A pure liar

Doing better
Aimed for peace
My simple words
True release

I try today
For tomorrow
Adding flowers
Fighting sorrow

Why can't you see
Are your eyes sad
Rinse them clean
Become most glad

Move for life now
Established limits
Real for others
Have no gimmicks

You can be free
With discipline
Answer to GOD
Developing kin

And then at night
When you're sleeping
Powerful dreams
Bring no weeping

Wake with a purpose
Coffee or work
Out of shadows
No longer lurk

With each handshake
Making connections
Positive future
Clear recollections

Alm #81

We have no job
We have no wife
We have no pride
We have a knife

Take up the knife
Cut an onion
Cook your dinner
Cross your canyon

Develop skills
Education
Seek solutions
Heal a nation

Bring yourself up
Fight to improve
Find a future
Make your move

Now have a job
But still no wife
A little pride
Sharpen your knife

Day after day
Punching the clock
Becoming better
Unlocking the lock

Keys to your life
Mark milestones
Chasing a love
Know in your bones

Flowers today
Lunch tomorrow
Pop the question
End your sorrow

Safe in your job
Now have a wife
Definitive joy
Buy a new knife

Alm #82

No one cares
And so you cry
No one cares
Until you die

You must try
Don't succumb
Take a breath
Overcome

For yourself
Be a good person
Be someone
And stop your cursin'

To give much
To succeed
Look ahead
For each need

Judging less
Giving more
Don't end up
On the floor

Look inside
Find a key

Live your life
Then you see

Goals achieved
Over time
Stop the tears
Stairs you climb

Day by day
Week by week
You will get
What you seek

In the end
You are free
Trust in GOD
You will see

Miracles
Daily love
With some hope
From above

Alm #83

Our lives
Earthquakes
We have made
Grave mistakes

We have been
Very low
Must now learn
How to grow

Find the fruit
Not the mold
Still have time
Young or old

Follow paths
Blaze anew
No more wrath
Left to chew

Look ahead
See the light
Be yourself
Find your might

As it goes
Three two one
Now let go
Light of sun

Picture true
Destiny
Pray to GOD
And be free

<u>Alm #84</u>

Rivers with rapids
Dangerous
Decisions made
Treacherous

Water gives life
Water brings death
So hold tight
Hold on to breath

Canoe is upright
Secure and afloat
Carry us through
Cross safely the mote

Paddle and steer
Wear safety vest
Realizing now
We are all blessed

Downstream it's calm
Is not far away
Stay in the boat
Try now to pray

Team work will help
Communication
Free dreams abound
Bringing elation

Adrenaline pumping
Scared by the rocks
White water rapids
Forget about clocks

Life is right now
Stay on the course
Rivers have glory
Rivers have force

Opening up
Calm just ahead
We made it through
Disregard dread

River now placid
Wide and relieved
Pain of your heart
No one believed

Safety is ours
Respite from fear
Thankful to GOD
Peace now is here

Alm #85

**Can't stand this pressure
Can't stand this pain
Oh where is the good
Oh where is the gain**

**Everything's rain
Torrential and grey
Lightning and thunder
This price that I pay**

**Don't go asunder
Don't fall to the ground
Steady your heartbeat
Let you be found**

**Agitated much
Seek out GOD's grace
Miracle of trust
Must steady your pace**

**Slow down a little
Please try to reflect
Forgive yourself now
Allow self-respect**

Voice from inside
Learn to discern
How to get by
From inside learn

Share it with others
See life aglow
Be rescued now
 Let yourself grow

Alm #86

Been paying off debts
Making improvements
Focused on future
Positive movements

Don't go with the tide
Be steadfast and strong
An anchor at sea
Face problems head-on

Times have been tougher
Like when you were young
Pray for forgiveness
GOD's ladder top rung

Solutions to issues
With earnest and haste
Offer ablutions
Do not be a waste

Fly like an eagle
Have sight and vision
Socially active
Face indecision

Aloft in the sky
See the big picture
Teach it to others
Offer a fixture

Must always remember
It takes effort to grow
Energize others
Help shovel their snow

Alm #87

This book is coming to an end
Yet for us it is just a beginning
Be the fruit of the flower of the tree
Envision yourself as always winning

Pace your heart and listen to your soul
Cards are being dealt as on we roll
See the ins and outs of every game
Once we wake prayer is our goal

Turn the dial and change the channel
What show you choose lights your candle
Be a beacon and lighthouse in the storm
Feel your way amidst Earthly swarm

Move yourself to the sun and the moon
Devastate never not even one room
Resolve problems head-on with a plume
Learn to know when to sweep with your broom

Finding GOD in your soul house
Hug another who walks without
Walk and talk to love and teach
Kiss the moments and hug and preach

Alm #88

Receive peace in GOD's time
Strive for every tomorrow
Climb mountains freeing thought
Emanate no sorrow

Laugh for every joy
Love a partner true
Have grace each day
Let happiness ensue

Open a new book
Writing your own verse
Lift yourself above
Any ancient curse

On holy sod we trod
Flag of freedom raise
Humble in uncertainty
Always offer praise

Remember to forgive
Sadness wash away
Never ending joy
Once again please pray

Invent your own mantra
Repeat it infinitely
Clear your soul of badness
Have solace definitively

And
As always

Praise
GOD

Nathaniel Schellhase Hvizdos

Nathaniel Schellhase Hvizdos

Special Props
To
Jeremy Frost

Nathaniel Schellhase Hvizdos

Nathaniel Schellhase Hvizdos

Nate holds the future as an opportunity to change for the better and to also help others to do the same in GOD's Way. His writing is meant for the benefit of others and to sway Light into places of darkness. He advises that this is the time of personal decisions and ultimately having to live with your decisions. Think, act, and reflect. There are no more excuses. Nate's aspires to truth and unity. His soundtrack is hardcore. What is yours? What do you want?

*Photo: Anna-Katya DeLorenzo Brue

Nathaniel Schellhase Hvizdos

Published by Greenback Books otherwise known as those writers who know nothing about publishing yet have friends who give tidbits of advice without committing to contracts or efforts to meet authors in the middle with their reasonable and mature requests for contractual agreements as a protection which causes the authors to rescind rights for the aforementioned to publish them resulting in run-on sentences like this showing zeal and attitude rejected by most professionals who elevate themselves erroneously to a stature above other humans which is vomitous and downright wrong as we are all people equal on the same level under GOD!!!

Nathaniel Schellhase Hvizdos

Nathaniel Schellhase Hvizdos

Made in the USA
Middletown, DE
03 May 2024